The Quick Guide to

Cocker Spaniel Puppies

Blair Smart

Copyright © 2014 by Blair Smart

All rights reserved.

No part of this book may be reproduced in any form or by any electronic or mechanical means, including information storage and retrieval systems, without prior permission of the publisher and author.

While attempts have been made to verify information contained in this publication, neither the author nor the publisher assumes any responsibility for errors, omissions, interpretation or usage of the subject matter herein. This publication contains the opinions and ideas of its author and is intended for informational purposes only and is meant to be a general guide. It is not intended, nor should it be treated, as a definitive guide on health and wellness, nor should it be regarded as medical or nutritional advice for any dogs.

The author and publisher shall in no event be liable or be held responsible for any loss or other damages incurred from the usage of this publication, or for any health needs that may arise, and will not be responsible for any loss, claim or action from the information contained in this book.

Contents

Introduction

Cocker spaniels are lively and intelligent dogs who make lovely companions and family pets when they've been carefully trained and socialized as pups. They are a joy to look at and a pleasure to be with. Generally healthy, they have a life expectancy of 12 to 14 years, and remains one of the most popular AKC (American Kennel Club) breeds.

Cockers are chosen by many small-dog enthusiasts due to their cheerful disposition. They're easily trained with a bit of patience and perseverance on your part. The puppies are playful, trustworthy and adaptable. They will thrive among groups of playing children and they may excel in obedience, agility and simple tricks.

Maybe you think of Lady from the movie *Lady and the Tramp* when you think of cocker spaniels. They certainly have the traits as portrayed in the

7

movie, such as loyalty, sweetness and eagerness to play. Their friendliness, devotion and ability to adapt to different environments and people make them a very popular breed to own.

Throughout the book, we are using the term "he" to avoid the clumsy use of "he or she". Your puppy is certainly not an "it"!

If you're thinking of introducing a cocker spaniel into your family, this book will provide you with all the essential information in every step from choosing a puppy to training and puppy care.

History of Breed

Cocker spaniels are descended from spaniels, an old breed of dog that has been famous throughout history by appearing in the stories of Chaucer and Shakespeare.

Spaniels are short-legged. They are small to medium-sized dogs with large drooping ears, feathered legs and tails, and usually long wavy hair.

While their origins are unknown, spaniels are commonly believed to come from Spain. They arrived in England during Caesar's invasion (54-55 BC), and this was when most of the spaniel breeds we know today began to take shape.

They were bred to flush game from dense bushes, and by the late 1600s, they've been trained into either water or land breeds. For example, the now extinct English water spaniel used to retrieve water fowls that their owners shot down with arrows.

In the 17th century, Englishmen began hunting with flintlock guns, and the role of the spaniel changed as they became posh gun dogs.

One type of land spaniel is the springing spaniel. They sprang pheasants, partridges and rabbits. Springing spaniel laid the foundation for modern day spaniels. One litter of Spring spaniels could produce three types of dogs, the main difference being their size. Larger pups remained springer spaniels, while medium-sized ones were called Sussex spaniels, and the smaller ones became cocker spaniels.

They were hard to categorize in shows. The pups could enter as cockers one year and turn into springers the next year when they grow up.

The cocker spaniel was finally recognized as a separate and distinct breed in 1892 by the Kennel Club of England.

Not long before, spaniels were introduced to America.

Spaniels were great companions to American hunters. They hunted best when their masters gunned over them. The spaniel has talent with flushing pheasant and woodcock, as well as grouse. They use their sense of smell to cover low areas, and their eyes and nose to locate the game once they are down.

American cocker spaniels are bred more for showing rather than hunting. They are a bit different in appearance than English cocker spaniels, who resembled their springer spaniel ancestors. American cockers are smaller, have a domed head, a shorter back and a shorter muzzle. The English version is taller, with a narrower head and chest.

American cocker spaniels garnered admiration from the world for the first time when one became the first of its breed to win Best in Show at the Westminster Kennel Club Dog Show in 1921. But as its popularity grew, puppy mills began breeding so-called cockers in unsafe, careless, and unethical ways. Once happy and healthy, they became plagued with hereditary diseases, particularly eye disorders. Temperament problems also introduced the term "cocker rage" to common use. They can also suffer from hip dysplasia.

English cockers on the other hand remained unchanged over the years, and health and temperament are not as much of an issue.

Today, there are two types of cocker spaniels: the show-type and the working type. While the show cockers are rarely trained nowadays, they still retain many of their hunting instincts.

In many archived photos and illustrations, cocker spaniels are shown with docked tails, which are tails that are half or two-thirds removed. Breeders used to use a sharp pair of shears to remove the tail. This was to prevent injury when the dogs ran to flush game.

If you decide that cocker spaniels are for you, it's essential to get them from a reputable breeder. The breeder will usually allow you to meet your puppy's relatives so you can see whether they are nervous or aggressive, and how they will develop.

It's important to maintain a good relationship with the breeder after the sale in case you need follow-up advice.

Physical Attributes

Cocker spaniels are the smallest of the sporting dog groups. Breed standards can vary from country to country. For example, the ideal height for a male cocker in the U.K. and the U.S. differs by an inch or two. You can get the breed standards from the Kennel Clubs of various countries.

COAT

The cocker's coats can be a variety of colors— from black to red to gold. No other breed can offer such a large variety to choose from. Sometimes they can be black and tan, liver and tan, and other mixtures including roans, tricolors, or solid colors with additional white markings. The dense coating provides protection from the elements, while the hair on their heads are short and fine. Feathering may appear on their ears, legs, chest and belly.

The coat itself can be silky, flat or slightly wavy. It keeps them warm in cold weather and prevents them from overheating in the summer. They love being outside.

When dogs have endearing orange patches above their eyes, it's believed in ancient folklore in Tibet that it gives the dogs magical powers of perception; they can warn their owners of impending doom or disaster!

BODY

Cockers have a compact and sturdy body, and despite their small size, they are capable of considerable speed and endurance. Although it's not always evident, a fully grown cocker is a muscular hunting dog, and their extensive muscle structure is concealed by a lush and beautiful coat.

The cocker's back evenly slops towards the tail, the hips are wide, and the rib cage is large. They possess a typical sporting gait, which requires good balance.

EYES

Their large brown eyes usually convey an intelligent, alert and soft expression.

MOUTH

Cockers have a strong jaw. They have teeth with scissor bite, which means that the teeth of the upper jaw closely overlaps the teeth in the lower jaw.

EARS

The size and shape of their ears give this breed its overall character. They are wide, long, oval in shape and well-feathered. When the ears are pulled forward, the ends should reach the tip of the dog's nose.

NECK

Their necks are long enough to allow him to sniff the ground easily, a must for any hunting dog.

HEADS

Differences between American and English cockers are not always obvious to the novice. English cockers are slightly larger than their American counterparts, but the most obvious difference is in the head shapes. American cockers have a distinctly domed skull and their lips tend to hang down farther and more loosely. Also, their eyes are slightly larger, and their coats are more profuse compared to their English cousins.

TAIL

The tail is set a little lower than the back. It should always be happily wagging in action.

Docking the tails of cocker spaniels is still a controversial issue. It's argued that working dogs can suffer tail damage if left undocked, but there might be health and psychological consequences. It's in the best interest of your dog to allow him to keep his natural tail. However, it is customarily docked for working dogs.

FEET & LEGS

Their legs are strong and muscular with good bones. They are short below the hocks on the hind legs to allow tireless movement. Their feet are neat, compact and cat-like.

MALE DOGS

When you're buying a male puppy, it's not always possible for their testicles to both come down together. They appear over a period of weeks or even months. Get your vet to check it out if you are in doubt. A male dog should have two testicles fully descended into the scrotum. A monorchid (only one testicle) or having one testicle retained inside the body can cause problems in the future.

Behavior

The cocker spaniel is happy and friendly. He is eager to please and a great companion. However, the occasional cocker showed temper problems in the 1930s. Some of them can be inflicted with a degree of so-called "rage syndrome", where they tend to bark in anger.

This behavior is not typical, but it can be provoked by a visitor or it can be spontaneous. How you take care of your dog as a young pup can have tremendous influence on his behavior. By holding, comforting and supporting him, he will feel more secure. They love cuddles and being stroked. If they are injured or in pain in any way, they will trust you to allow you to take care of them.

Be prudent of any rage problems before buying your puppy or dog. Only a small percentage suffer from rage problems. Sometimes they are nervous and might misinterpret the movements of the owner and the family members. An unbalanced dog might feel as if they need to defend themselves or feel confused and afraid. Watch his facial expressions and be in tune with his body language so that you can be one step ahead of him.

Pros and Cons of a Cocker Spaniel

The fun and satisfaction that comes with owning a cocker spaniel puppy outweighs the disadvantages, but you should be aware of all the pros and cons of owning this breed:

PROS:

Cocker spaniels are sweet-natured, obedient, devoted and friendly. They adapt well to new people and environments, and they do not bark excessively, which makes them suitable for small living spaces such as apartments.

They are generally happy and receptive to positive reinforcements. They are popular dogs that do well in a family of any size due to their good nature.

Cocker spaniels generally get along with children as long as the children play with them calmly. Older children love cocker spaniels because they are eager to please. They're alert and affection, ready to obey your command.

They generally enjoy a long life—up to 15 years.

CONS:

Cockers need lot of mental and physical stimulation, so you must take him out to exercise often.

Since their ears are prone to infection, you must check and clean them often.

The coats of show type dogs can grow quickly and it can take a bit of work to make the coat look good.

They can get aggressive if they are not trained and socialized properly.

They are highly social animals, so make sure you have have plenty of time to devote to him! A cocker can develop behavioural problems if left on their own often, and they shouldn't be left alone for long periods of time. They are not suitable for owners who are at work all day.

Where to Buy Your Puppy

When you take on a new puppy, you will be sharing your life with him for the next twelve or so years. Many people are not aware of the responsibilities involved in dog ownership, therefore please carefully consider whether you have the time and energy required for this breed.

When you do decide that cocker spaniels are for you, it's important to take the trouble to research and find the most reliable sources.

Buy your puppy from reputable breeders. There are hobby dog breeders who breed the occasional litter with the aim of producing good show and working dogs, or the large scale breeder that specialize in one breed only. Buying from a hobby dog breeder is ideal because the puppies will be house reared and they will be with their mother. There would probably be more human handling, which would help them get used to human presence.

Local dog shows are worth visiting because you can check out a number of cockers. If you watch the judging, you can get an idea of the dogs that appeal to you. You will also be able to meet some exhibitors and breeders. Buy a catalogue of the show. It will give you the names and addresses of all the exhibitors. Walk around the benching area where the dogs are waiting to be shown and sometimes there may be a sign that puppies are expected shortly from various kennels.

Your vet is a good source for recommending local breeders. You may also try your friends and personal contacts for recommendations.

You may also try breed rescue centers, but this is usually for older dogs. Dogs can be rescued for a variety of reasons. Sometimes it's due to the death of the owner, but most of the time the previous owner was unable to deal with the dog who may now have developed some difficult habits. The first-time owner would be best to start with a puppy because obtaining a dog from a rescue center would need lots of patience and animal understanding. But of course, it can also be rewarding.

Tips for Choosing a Puppy

Now that you've identified where to buy your puppy, it's helpful to make a list of questions and concerns you want to bring up when you visit the breeder. A good breeder will also have a number of questions for you before an agreement can be reached.

What to ask:

• Ask for a puppy diet sheet since puppies are gradually weaned from their mother's milk by five to six weeks of age.

• Details of pedigree.

• Make sure that the litter has been recorded by the breeder with the Kennel Club. If it isn't, you will be unable to transfer the ownership of your dog officially to your name, and you won't be able to show the dog in your own name.

• Tactfully enquire about any inherited diseases or problems. Has his parents been examined or tested? Most breeders will provide this information without being asked.

• Get a firm agreement on the price for the puppy. Make sure to get a receipt for your purchase.

Questions you may be asked:

• Caring breeders will want to know that there is someone at home to be with the dog in the daytime, or whether work facilities are appropriate for the dog to go to.

• They'll want to know whether you have a safe garden, or at least an area which is fenced off where the puppy cannot escape.

Watch the puppies. Don't buy puppies that look thin, unhappy, and perhaps showing evidence of discharge from the eyes or ears. Their coats should be smooth and shiny, and the eyes should be bright and have a friendly expression. The nose of a healthy cocker is usually wet, but not running.

The mother should look well fed and cared for. Talk to her gently. (If she greets you by lying submissively on her back and urinating a little, this is a sign of nervousness and not a good one. This is not the usual behavior of a merry cocker, even if she is protective of her pups.)

Play with the puppy. Stroke him and let him get used to your scent.

All puppies are cute and cuddly, but select the puppy that is suited to your lifestyle. If you watch the litter carefully, you will see subtle differences from one puppy to the next. Some will be bolder than others. If you have an active family lifestyle, you may want to choose a livelier puppy. If you lead a quiet life, then perhaps a calmer puppy is for you.

Male or Female?

If you are getting a cocker strictly as a pet, note that female cockers are slightly smaller and more sedate. They can be a little more affectionate and sensitive than their male counterparts, who are a bit more independent. These differences may not be that noticeable unless you own a male and a female at the same time.

The choices of sex is more important if you plan on becoming a breeder. Of course you would want a female. However, if you decide to get a female cocker but don't plan to breed her, you should have her spayed to reduce the risk of ailments such as breast tumors, ovarian cysts and false pregnancies. You would also avoid the messiness that may occur when she is in season.

Housing and Supplies

Here are some essential equipment you'll need to prepare to welcome the new pup into your home:

- Puppy pen/bed
- Bed with washable pad
- Toys
- Collar and leash
- Feeding bowls
- Puppy Food
- Grooming equipment (See Puppy Care chapter)

Eating and Sleeping

Cocker spaniels will require a space to call their own. Fortunately, because they are small, they don't require a big territory as larger breeds do. By choosing the eating or sleeping places that give your beloved a sense of security, you will prevent undue stress on him and help him avoid the physical and behavior problems associated with a tense and unhappy animal.

First, they need a feeding and sleeping area indoors, which gives them a place of refuge to rest when they need to.

Find a place that will be comfortable for your beloved puppy. This means a room that doesn't have heavy human traffic, but not so isolated that it would be difficult for him to make contact with people. Choose a room where the dog can be easily confined when you go to sleep or go out. A corner of a room is preferable, as the dog is protected on two sides, and this would give him a sense of security. Avoid placing the bed in a drafty room, or one where he would be exposed to direct sunlight.

Since puppies tend to be destructive in the first few months while they are teething, you may want to delay purchasing a real dog bed. Even strong plastic and nylon types can become ragged after some time in the company of your new friend! You can use cardboard boxes from the supermarket covered with a pillow case. Place a sleeping pad inside. When you do buy a bed, it needs to be washable.

As cockers feel more secure in confined areas, they take to cages or a restricted pen. If you don't want to use a cage, a sleeping box or a sleeping basket works well.

Feed your pup in a room that is easily cleaned, like a kitchen. It's important that he can be left in peace to eat in this area, because nervous dogs can have trouble digesting food properly.

Backyard Safety

Puppies love being outside, but make sure that your backyard is one where a small puppy cannot escape. Wooden fences or strong wire mesh fencing can be used, and remember to keep gates closed. Sometimes puppies can slip under certain gates, so add more mesh to the bottom to prevent this if necessary.

If your garden is large, you might want to make a small area dog-proof and allow him to be in the rest of the garden only when you are present. It's best to connect this dog-proof area to the back door/house.

If there is a pond in the garden, cover it to avoid accidents. Remove any chemicals and insecticides that can cause serious harm to dogs. If you use them, keep them under lock and key in a garden shed.

If you know that your grass and herbs have not been chemically sprayed, you can allow your pup to eat them when they seek them out. Sometimes dogs will choose the grasses that will make him vomit because there may be unhealthy irritants in his stomach that will be brought up at the same time as the grass. This is fine.

However, many garden bulbs, shrubs and plants are poisonous to dogs. Puppies seldom have the sense to leave them alone, but some do have the instinct to do so. Beware of: azalea, arrow grove, bayonet root, burning bush leaves, cyclamen, caster beans, dumb cane weed, hemlock, elephant bar, foxglove, jimson weed, laburnum, lily of the valley, locowed, mistletoe, monkshead roots, mock orange blossom, narcissus bulbs, peach, elderberry, cherry trees (bark), pimpernel, poinsettia, rhodo-dendron leaves, rhubarb leaves, sweet pa (stem), scotch broom seeds, tulip bulbs, and wisteria.

Toys

Toys are important in keeping your dog physically and mentally fit. Cocker spaniel puppies love to play and they're quickly stimulated by toys. Chewable toys made from tough rubber-type material is ideal for the play pen. They will want to chew on these for hours.

Nylon chew bones and toys are also great to keep their teeth clean and healthy; they're a great help to teething puppies.

They love to chase balls out into the yard, but make sure to use a well-made ball that is solid and too large to swallow. They particularly like to have a favorite toy to carry in their mouths to "offer" you to welcome your return. If you don't give them one, they'll find "offerings" of their own, such as tea-towels, shoes, or anything else they can find! They have a natural carrying instinct, so allow them to exercise it. You can even make your own with some old socks that have been washed and stuffed tightly full of other socks and then knotted or sewn up at the top. This costs nothing and they love it.

Tug toys made from knotted rope are fun for two dogs to play together.

Frisbees can also be fun when your puppy gets older. It will help him be adept at direction and catching.

Collars and Leashes

For the puppy's first collar, a soft leather collar is a good choice. However, it's not worth buying a pricey one because he will grow out of it very quickly. Alternatively, a nylon ribbon-type is fine.

Invest in a good leather leash. Your puppy won't outgrow it and it will become supple and pleasant for you to use in time. Its clip is important and should be examined before purchase to make sure that it is sturdy and won't release by itself. You may find rope leashes to be slippery and less comfortable on the hand.

An extending leash is very useful in training your dog. It gives him the additional space to run while you still have control of the leash.

Feeding Bowls

Small bowls with sloping sides are good because they avoid getting the food all over your pet's ears at meal times. Certain ceramic oval pie dishes are helpful for small pups as well.

Have clean drinking water available at all times. The best drinking bowl to use is a plastic type with a fitted lid that leaves only a small drinking space in the center with enough room for the face but not the ears.

Identification

Get a disc engraved now and attach it to your puppy's collar as soon as possible.

An alternative and more or less permanent way of identification is by tattoo. This can be done on the hairless inside flap of the ear or inside a back leg. This can be done a tattooist who does not need veterinary qualifications.

Preparing for Your Puppy's Arrival

If it's possible, visit your puppy a few times before you bring him home so that he becomes familiar with your presence. Your puppy will be less stressed if he recognizes a friendly face when he finds himself in a new environment.

Prepare the housing for your new pup, as well as the supplies. Find out what kind of food he likes from the breeder or a pet shop manager and buy a supply ahead of time.

Purchase all the equipment and accessories and find a place in your house to store them.

Make sure to "puppy-proof" you house. You can do this by removing all sharp objects such as staples, nails and broken glass from every nook and cranny of your house. Make sure that all electrical cords and wires are out of his reach. Place paints, disinfectants, insecticides, cleaners, anti-freeze, etc. in a location that your puppy can't access. A young dog is very inquisitive and will use its nose to sniff, his paws to touch and his teeth to chew everything he comes across.

Don't forget to check your backyard, garage, and any other spaces that your puppy might pass. If you're unsure whether something will be harmful to him, clear it to be on the safe side.

Advise your family and friends on how to handle a new cocker puppy with these tips:

• While you might be excited about your puppy's arrival and want to invite everyone over to see him, hold off on it at first. Let your puppy adjust to you and your family first before subjecting him to strangers.

• Handle your new puppy gently. They are fragile creatures and need to be handled with care until they grow larger. Advise your children not to poke or prod the puppy, probe his ears, or subject him to any other types of rough handling.

• The proper technique to lift a puppy is to place one hand under the puppy's chest while the other hand is placed under him to support its rear end and hind legs. Never pick up a puppy by the neck or with one hand under the abdomen, as these methods can hurt him.

• Allow your puppy to walk as much as possible, so avoid picking him up too much. He will need exercise and develop confidence in his own physical abilities.

• Don't give him bones or very hard objects. A puppy under 6 months old only has its milk teeth and cannot chew hard objects.

• Don't place your puppy on counters, tables or beds and subject him to unnecessary heights.

• Try not to leave your puppy unsupervised in the first few weeks.

Before the arrival of your new cocker spaniel puppy, decide where he will sleep. Prepare a nice warm bed, a cuddle toy, dim lighting and a radio. If you have neighbours, warn them of your puppy's arrival. He might wake you up the first few nights, but don't get cross with him—he is in a new place and he might be frightened because he has never been alone before.

Pick a place for him to sleep and stick to it. They usually settle in quicker if you keep them near you. If this is not possible, simply be patient.

Set rules from day one and stick to them. This can mean preventing your pup from jumping on the furniture, to begging for scraps. See your pup as a blank canvas. If you don't want your adult cocker spaniel to do things such as jumping on your houseguest, prevent them from doing so when they are young.

Reward their good behavior, and allow them to learn. Remember that they are still learning your language and the more you praise them, the quicker they will learn.

Find a good vet for you cocker spaniel. They are generally healthy, but they need immunization after arriving in your home, as well as routine healthcare checkups throughout their lives.

Welcoming Your Puppy Home

When you go to pick up your new puppy from the pet store or the breeder, don't forget to bring a collar, leash and traveling cage with you so that he won't be loose in your car on the journey home, even if you are only traveling a short distance.

Take the travel cage with you and leave it for a short time in his familiar play area to allow his mom and other puppies to sniff in and around it. The box will have the friendly smell he is used to when he goes with you in the car.

Make sure that the cage will not move at all during the journey. If it does take some time to get home, be prepared if your puppy gets carsick. It will probably be the first time that he has been in a car and he may not be very happy about it. Line the traveling cage with blankets in case of accidents.

Have a towel and a short-bristle brush to clean him, but avoid using water as that can cause a chill.

Reassure the puppy and comfort him to help him settle in. Don't leave him on his own to cry.

Let your puppy walk around outside when you've reached home. Take him to an area you've chosen where he can relieve himself.

In the first few days, keep your visitors to a minimum. Introduce him to his new family before neighbours and friends. You little friend might be a bit apprehensive and scared being away from his mother and siblings, so make sure that he's protected from additional stress in a calm atmosphere. Reassure him that he will be safe and loved in his new home.

Introduce him to his safe den space and interest him in a toy. Play with him. If you have other pets in the house, let them wait to meet him until your new puppy is asleep. Then they can come in and sniff around. Older pets might get jealous of a new puppy, so let them get to know each other slowly. Don't leave them alone together until you're sure that it's safe.

Puppy Care

Don't leave your new friend home alone for long periods of time, especially in the first few days, because it will cause unnecessary emotional stress. If you have to leave, ask a relative or trusted friend to watch him, preferably at home.

After a few weeks, your new pup will feel completely at ease in your home after having gained your confidence and trust. You can try to leave him for longer periods of time, but still limit his access to his sleeping and feeding areas. When you do leave, inspect your home to catch any potential hazards that might harm your puppy.

For a clean and well-groomed cocker, you'll need the following supplies and equipment:

- Wide and fine toothed comb,

- Soft-bristled brush

- Pin-headed brush

• Thinning scissors and pointed end scissors

• Nail clippers

• Toothbrush

• Stripping comb

• Puppy shampoo

• Ear cleaning solution

• Cotton balls

• Cotton swabs

• Soap

• Sink spray hose

Grooming

The cocker's coat is dense and of medium length to protect him from the elements. His coat must be maintained in top condition.

While he's still a puppy, you can teach him to enjoy the grooming routine with daily brushing and stroking sessions. Use the brush that you've specified from you pet shop or vet that is best for your cocker spaniel. Comb or brush in the direction in which the hair lies. Brushing removes dead hair and scurf but also stimulates the sebaceous glands to produce the natural oils that keep the coat glossy and healthy.

By his sixth month, his coat will grow, and additional attention to grooming is needed. Stand him on a table with a matte surface so that he feels secure and will not slip.

Follow these five grooming tips to ensure a good experience for the both of you:

Step 1: Since his ears can become matted and tangled, start by carefully parting them with your fingers. Use a wide-toothed comb to gently comb down from the head to the ear tip. Keep the neck under the ear trimmed with thinning scissors.

Make sure that when you are trimming the hair short under the ear that you don't accidentally nip the sensitive folds of his skin.

Step 2: Take the soft bristle brush to brush down the length of his body for a few minutes in the direction you want the coat to lie. This will encourage a shining coat. Use a wide-toothed comb to comb the hair down the chest, and under the tail and legs.

Step 3: Trim excess hair around each foot, then trim the hair between the toes. Leave enough hair underneath the pads for protection.

Step 4: Darker colored cockers usually have a heavier coat. Occasional use of a stripping knife may be justified. Use it to remove excess whiskers on the face if they are growing towards the eyes, but don't remove the sensor whiskers, which he uses to test width.

Step 5: With a finger and thumb, remove the few stray hairs that may grow in excess at the top of your dog's head.

If you want to use a professional groomer, say every four months, look for someone who can trim or strip a cocker by hand. Electric clippers, used by many grooming parlors, might ruin its natural coat, and should not be used if you ever plan to show your dog.

Cutting Toe Nails

Use the nail clippers at a correct angle to trim the toe nails. Ask your vet or a professional groomer to show you how to do this for the first time. Take off a little rather than too much at first. Light colored nails are easier to cut because you can see the quick outlined and avoid it. Black nails are more difficult, so don't do it yourself if you are unsure how to go about this.

Mouth

Use a special toothpaste for dogs from your vet or the pet store on a weekly basis to help maintain healthy teeth and gums, as well as avoiding bad breath and removing dental plaque.

Ears

Wash your hands with soap and dry them to make sure that any bacteria on your hands won't be transferred to your puppy's ears. Sit in a chair and hold your puppy. Your ear cleaning solution, cotton swabs, and cotton balls should be within reach.

Pour the ear cleaning solution on a cotton ball. Lift up the first ear and wipe the cotton ball from the inside out to clean any wax and debris. Dip a cotton swab into the solution. Gently hold his ear and wipe the cotton swab along the ridges. Don't push the buds down into the ear.

Repeat this process with a new cotton ball and swab for the other ear.

Baths

Some cocker spaniel puppies might take to water right away, while others will try to escape. At first, the water and puppy shampoo may get everywhere, but the experience will improve with each bath.

First, brush you puppy with the soft-bristled brush to remove tangles, dirt and debris, followed by a de-matting comb if necessary.

Fill a sink up to 4 inches of lukewarm water. Place your puppy in the water and spray him with the sink hose spray to wet him thoroughly. To wet his stomach and underside, lift him up with one hand under his chest. Pour a ribbon of puppy shampoo along his back and lather by rubbing it into his fur. Work from head to tail.

Rinse him thoroughly with lukewarm water from the hose once again. Make sure all the shampoo is off his skin because it can cause extreme itching and discomfort. Keep rinsing until the water runs clear off your little guy, and turn the faucet off.

Release the sink stopper. Let the water drain.

Remove him from the sink onto a towel. Fold the towel up around him to dry him, although he'll probably shake as soon as you stop drying him to remove additional water.

Let him run around and roll or dry for a while until he calms down.

Wipe clean the excess water on the floor and surrounding surfaces.

After each cleaning process, give your dog a treat, a hug and plenty of praise for his patience and good behavior!

Development

Dogs are considered puppies from birth to one year of age. When they are newborns, they are blind, deaf and toothless. The can't regulate body temperature, urinate or defecate on their own. They are dependent on their mother and siblings for warmth, huddling close together to conserve body temperature.

In the second week of life, eyes and ears that have been sealed from birth begin to open. They learn what their mother looks like and begin to "speak" by expanding their grunts to yelps, whines and barks.

After the second week, they can usually stand, and by day 21, they will take their first unsteady walk.

It's not a good idea to visit puppies when they are this young. There's a small risk of infection and some mothers are protective towards the puppies.

In week three, they continue to develop physically and sensorily. They grow a little more independent from their mothers and will begin to play with the other pups.

When he is first brought home, no changes should be made to his breeder's diet sheet. It's common that he will eat four meals a day at this age, but three meals will suffice at four months old. A puppy's stomach is small and he can't take in sufficient nutrients to grow unless he is fed little and often.

They can control their bladders at around 6 weeks of age. Cocker spaniel puppies are too young to be potty trained until 8 weeks old. See the Training chapter to potty train your pet.

At 3 to 4 months old, this is a time when your puppy is like a toddler. He might begin ignoring commands he has already learned just like a child does when they're exerting their independence. Gentle but firm reinforcement of training and commands will help.

At around 4 months old, they will shed the little teeth that they are born with. The transition from temporary to permanent teeth should be complete by the time they are 6 months old. See your vet if the teeth seem out of position or if there are extra teeth present.

Around 3 to 5 months old, puppies will often bite and become bossy and assertive. They grow out of this phase as long as they are properly treated and not given power to dominate over the human family members.

If the pup bites you, a sharp "No!" or "No biting!" command, then ignoring him briefly should improve this.

You can play with your dog, but avoid games like tug of war or wrestling. The games can get out of hand and if he wins, he might perceive it as an act of dominance. When he grows stronger, he'll want to continue to play-fight to see who is stronger. Don't fight because otherwise he'll think that fighting you is permissible.

Fetch, sniff-out-the-treat, hide-and-seek, leash training and other mild mannered games is preferred to train your dog.

At 4 to 6 months old, your puppy will test you more to exercise his independence. He might teeth during this time and will want to chew on things. Giving him frozen doggie bones can help soothe his pain and relieve pressure.

Your pup might try to assert his dominance over your family, especially the children. Don't let him off his leash during this period unless you are in a confined space. Continue training him in obedience and basic commands.

He might ignore your commands to return, and if you let him loose in public, it will greatly increase his chances of injury or even death, so be careful and don't take the chance.

He'll go through hormonal changes, and you should get him neutered or sprayed if you have a female.

It's important to cure your puppy of biting and aggression before the fifth month. The longer he retains his bad behavior, the harder it will be to break.

They should be hand-fed by all members of the family, and taught to accept food slowly and graciously. Don't let them snap and lunge for the food.

Don't leave you beloved home alone. Dogs in general are highly social pack animals and crave contact. Solitary confinement kills their zest for life! They will suffer very much if left alone, and may end up going to the toilet in the house due to being shut up. His distress can be intense, so arrange for a friend or neighbour to come and play with him if you're going to be out running errands for a couple of hours. Exercise him well before you go and leave him with his favorite toys.

Training

Potty Training

Every time he wakes up, and after every meal, he will want to urinate. Set his habits by taking him to a chosen spot in the garden if it's not wet or cold outside, or place him on some paper. Letting your puppy use newspaper in the house is a quick house-training method.

To ensure the training's success, always wait with him until he goes and praise him after. Your pup will learn fast if you are patient with him.

At eight weeks, a young pup has a small bladder and needs to empty himself every few hours, so there's bound to be some messes here and there. Don't scold him after or you will confuse him and training will be more difficult. If you catch him in the act, you can say "no" and carry him to the approved spot.

If you're watchful, you'll pick up the signals that he wants to relieve himself. He'll sniff the ground and rush about. Take him out to his spot at once before it's too late.

Using a neutralizing disinfectant in the house to clean up accidents can prevent your puppy from returning and using it as his favorite spot.

Hands-on Training

It's important that your puppy learn to love your hands, so never use them to punish him. Stroke and reward him—stroking your dog has been proven to improve your health as well!

Many dogs are touch-sensitive and they will be mesmerized by being stroked. He'll love it so much that he'll do anything you want as long as he understands your commands.

The secret to successful training is kindness and reward. However don't overfeed him with treats. Once in a while will suffice.

Stick with calling him by one name. He will get used to the sound of it and will have the need to respond when you call him. Say his name in a pleasant voice. If you must say "no", don't use his name, ie, don't say "No, Sammy". He'll associate it with having done something wrong.

"Sit"

An easy trick to get him to sit is to tell him to sit just he is about to do so. Gently hold him there in the sitting position as you repeat "sit" and praise him in a pleasant voice. Teaching him to do what he was about to do anyway is a great method to train him quickly.

"Come"

Teach "come" in the same manner—when he comes to you. Use his name. Make it a game by stepping back a little. Don't fall into the trap of chasing him when you want him to come, or you'll teach him to run away when you use this command.

Before you call him to eat, let him see his bowl and tell him to "come" so he associates this command with something he likes.

Leash and Collar Training

While dogs don't like being restrained by leashes and collars, it's necessary to make it safe to take them outside. Allow your puppy to get familiar with his collar and leash. Be patient.

In the first few days, put on his collar and let him drag it around for a minute or two so he can get used to it. When you are walking him, don't drag him if he is reluctant to walk.

Once he has gotten accustomed to walking with you, you can use an extending leash to give him space to roam. Just make sure that he is obedient and reliable before you allow him to do so.

He should walk on your left side with a slack leash. You can encourage this with a toy or a small treat in your left hand.

If he pulls you one way, don't tug him back. Call his name instead and turn and walk in the direction you want to go. Reward and praise him when he responds correctly.

Once he's able to walk on a leash, you can take him to the park where he can encounter other dogs, people and situations.

Punishment

Saying "no, bad dog" in a firm voice is enough to correct most dogs. Most experts believe that hitting, bullying and teasing will destroy the affectionate relationship between owner and dog. A confident dog is a happy dog. Cuddles, strokes and massages at grooming time will keep him happy.

If you must punish him, you can ignore him for a short period of time, but only when you've made it clear that he has done something wrong. Say "no" and briefly ignore him. Do not use this punishment often as it would wound him.

Bad Habits

If your puppy is teething, he might get very destructive. Or he might simply be destructive when he is bored. The solution is to play with him well, or give him enough exercise time before you go out, and then place him in his sleeping area with his toys.

Avoid feeding him scraps of your dinner. This practice has great potential for teaching your cocker puppy some bad habits, such as begging. On that note, never feed him pork that is not completely cooked, and also avoid feeding him pieces of chicken with bones in them.

Training Classes

If you wish, you can sign your pet up for formal training classes. Visit the class first without your puppy to get a feel for the atmosphere and to make sure that it is a positive experience. Dog trainers and their methods vary, so check them out before you commit.

Socialization

Socializing your puppy properly is important because poor socialization is the top cause of canine aggression and other bad behaviors. The advantage of a socialized dog is that they rarely bite and are less aggressive.

Ask your vet when you should take your puppy out to mix and socialize with other dogs and people. They can usually do so after they've completed vaccination. Usually this is before the age of 12 weeks.

Puppies spend 3 to 5 weeks of critical socializing time with the breeder, so be sure to purchase your cocker from a reputable breeder who socializes them well. Good breeders will also give you a detailed socialization regime to follow.

The breeder has a lot of responsibility because they select the father and mother to produce and ensure the cocker puppies of the best temperament. But temperament is also determined by environmental factors. Some experts say that 40% of their temperament is due to socialization and training, and 60% is inherited.

Check if there is a puppy play group in your area. If there is, don't take him until you have visited and feel that the puppies are happy and having fun. Don't cause him stress by exposing him to harsh treatment or even harsh voices. If the puppy group is good, he'll have a fun and useful experience. This can be very helpful so that your puppy has the interactive skills when you take him to the park where there are other dogs.

Once your puppy has settled in your home and trusts you, visitors of all ages can be allowed. Don't let them encourage too much boisterous behavior from your dog. Make sure that children don't tease or pester the puppy. There should be adult supervision at all times when the children are playing with your puppy.

Expose your puppy to the domestic sounds of your house, such as the vacuum cleaner, hair dryer, washing machines and other noisy items. Don't make an issue of them. Your pup should gradually get used to them. If you'd like, you can use a sound CD to play common noises in the household and the environment, including thunder, fireworks, fire trucks and children playing and screaming.

The puppy will learn to accept the noises and filter them out when he hears them repeatedly.

Common Ailments

Many cocker spaniel health problems can be avoided by giving your puppy a healthy diet, weekly grooming, lots of exercise, and regular health checkups at the vet. Keep a watchful eye on your dog to nip any problems in the bud.

Some of the typical hereditary health problems that this breed might face are:

- Glaucoma

- Cataracts

- Progressive Retinal Atrophy (PRA)

- Familial Nephropathy (Fatal Kidney Disease)

- Hip Dysplasia (Abnormal Development of the Hip Joint)

- Auto-Immune Disease

- Allergies

Responsible, reputable breeders test their dogs prior to breeding to ensure that their puppies will be strong, so make sure to buy your puppy from a good breeder.

Cocker spaniels have long beautiful ears, but they don't always allow enough air to circulate around its entrance, plus they tend to grow hair around the opening of the ear canal that further restricts the air. This dark, moist place can be a breeding ground for bacteria, therefore, cocker spaniels can be more prone to ear infections than other breeds. This can be quite a painful and uncomfortable experience for your dog.

If left untreated, this can result in eventual deafness, so it's very important to clean your dog's ears regularly to fight any infection and excess bacteria.

Keep the hair trimmed around the inside of his ears and check the ears once a week for signs of an ear infection. This only takes a couple of minutes.

Signs of an ear infection:

• The insides are inflamed or swollen.

• You smell a foul odour emanating from the ears.

• His ears are sensitive or tender.

• There is a dark, odorous discharge.

• Your dog shakes his head, tilts his head to one side, and rubs his ears along the ground more often than usual.

• He scratches his ears often.

• Your pet has haematomas (blood blisters) or melanomas (tumours).

• His behavior changes (depression, irritability).

If you do discover any of these signs, don't clean them away. If you do, you'll make it harder for you vet to diagnosis the problem since you will have removed the visible evidence of infection.

If your pet runs daily or swims often, you may need to check and clean his ears more often because his ears may pick up "nasties" that can cause irritation and infection.

It can take up to 6 months to clear up an ear infection.

If your dog is not used to the cleaning process, the following tips will help him get accustomed to having his ears handled:

• Gently massage and stroke your pup's ears. The more you handle his ears, the more he will get used to it.

• Praise him when he doesn't object. If he does, and you're sure you are not hurting him, don't stop. If you do, he'll squirm and resist more often if he sees that he can stop by doing so.

• If he continues to wiggle, distract him with a treat or a toy, and when he stops, praise him.

• Do this every day for a week or until he allows his ears to be handled without protest.

• The next step is to massage the inside of his ear gently with your clean fingertips.

For how to clean his ears, see the "Puppy Care" chapter.

Signs of a Healthy Puppy

A healthy puppy generally looks and acts healthy. He is eager to play with you, and as he is a working gun dog, he should be ready for walks and lots of exercise.

His eyes are bright and alert. Aside from a small amount of "sleep" in the inner corners of his eyes, there should be no discharge.

His nose is typically wet and cold with no discharge, but a little clear fluid is not uncommon.

The cocker's ears are sharp and responsive to the sounds around him. The inside of his ear flap is pale pink. There should be no visible wax and no unpleasant smells. He shouldn't be scratching his ears or shaking his head too much.

A healthy coat will be glossy and pleasant to the touch. He shouldn't scratch excessively. His coat can smell "doggy", but not too unpleasant. It's normal for him to shed hairs continuously to some degree. Groom him daily to keep him in first-class condition.

If his tail is docked, it will be one-quarter of its full length. If he is undocked, the tail will taper gradually and will be well feathered.

His teeth should be white and smooth. If they are yellow and dull, it might be tartar formation or plaque.

His claws should not be broken or too long. They should end at the ground, level with the pad. They have five toes on the front feet and four on the hind feet.

Depending on breed, diet, temperament and opportunity, he can pass stools between once to six times a day.

Being territorial, males urinate several times on a walk. Females do so a lot less.

In general, 60% of dogs are overweight. Don't let your cocker get obese. It's a health risk to dogs as it is to people. Have a monthly weigh-in for him to track our puppy's progress. A fully grown cocker should weigh around 26 lbs (12 kg). An easy way to weigh him is to weigh yourself first, then weigh yourself again holding your dog. Subtract your own weight from the latter result to get his weight.

He should be not too fat and not too thin. Balance the right amount of exercise with a healthy diet.

Show Requirements

Even the most experienced breeder will have a difficult time telling how a puppy will look as an adult. If you definitely want to show your dog, buy a cocker of at least nine months of age. This way, it's possible to see how the dog develops both in coat, movement and temperament. The older puppy will cost more because it will have been vaccinated, trained, reared and generally looked after by its breeder.

The standard of breeding is excellent nowadays and if you go to a reliable source, you'll be the proud owner of a beautiful cocker.

Each nation has its own set of breed standards. If you are showing your dog outside of the United States, ensure that it conforms to the official standard of the host country. Check with them, but for an overview for breed standards, see the "Physical Attributes" chapter of this book.

Cocker spaniels should be merry in nature with an ever-wagging tail. Their temperament is affectionate, yet full of life and exuberance. The eyes are dark brown or brown, and never light, though in some cases, hazel brown works with liver, liver roan, and liver and white coats.

Males should have two apparently normal testicles fully descended into the scrotum.

Any departures from the breed standard are considered faults. The seriousness with which the fault is regarded should be in exact proportion to its degree.

In general, the cocker spaniel is an attractive, active, merry sporting dog. The standard calls for a flat, silky textured coat with feathering on ears, legs and belly. How much feathering depends on the natural coat your dog is blessed with. If you've been grooming your dog daily, the effort required to groom your beloved for the show will be much easier.

Make sure the puppy is knot-free. His "fluff" should come out in the daily brushings. The best method to remove surplus hair is by the finger and thumb method. When you become proficient at this, it will not hurt your pet at all.

Do NOT pull his whiskers out however. It is very painful and you may alienate him. Using a sharp pair of scissors will cut the whiskers close to the short facial hair.

Don't remove your puppy's coat before it is loose enough to come out easily. It might break off halfway, or the coat will look "moth-eaten" with many bald patches. It can take several months to grow back, so do be patient for it to grow out naturally. Cocker puppies look great in their natural fluffy coats up the nine or ten months. The judges do not expect them to have a full coat at this stage. However, it is expected for their feet to be trimmed and for the excess hair on top of the head, ears and hocks to be removed.

Give him a bath about three days before the show. Don't dry him with rigorous rubbing. Squeeze and pat him to a damp state, and then comb out his legs, tummy and ears. Wrap and pin a towel around his middle. Now you can concentrate on drying his other areas. If you have a blowdryer, you will need someone to hold your pet while you proceed.

Make sure that the coat is dry to the skin and not just the top coat. After the four legs are dried, remove he towel. Direct the heat flow to the back and tummy. Once the tummy coat is dried, turn off the drier, brush the dog and if there are any loose ends, trim them off neatly.

Conclusion

Cocker spaniels puppies are adorable, lively, alert and intelligent. Be gentle and patient with him and he will reward you with his loyalty and eagerness to please.

Keep him in good health with regular checkups and daily grooming. His ears may need a bit more attention because they are prone to infection. Watch his weight and start training him immediately to form good behavior early on.

Get him socializing as soon as possible so he can learn to interact with other dogs and different people. It will tame his aggressive nature and he will bite less. Taking him to puppy socialization classes can be very beneficial, even if it means traveling the distance to get there.

Try not to leave your puppy alone, especially at first. Take care of him and train him with the tips in this book and he'll grow into a wonderfully happy and healthy dog who will be your most loyal friend.

Blair Smart

Printed in Great Britain
by Amazon